DOCUMENTING U.S. HISTORY

THE CIVIL WAR

THROUGH

PHOTOGRAPHY

Darlene R. Stille

Heinemann
LIBRARY

Chicago, Illinois

www.capstonepub.com
Visit our website to find out more information about Heinemann-Raintree books.

To order:
☎ Phone 800-747-4992
🖥 Visit www.capstonepub.com
to browse our catalog and order online.

© 2013 Heinemann Library
an imprint of Capstone Global Library, LLC
Chicago, Illinois

Edited by Abby Colich, Megan Cotugno, and Laura Hensley
Designed by Cynthia Della-Rovere
Original illustrations © Capstone Global Library
  Limited 2011
Illustrated by Oxford Designers & Illustrators
Picture research by Tracy Cummins
Originated by Capstone Global Library Limited
Printed and bound in China by CTPS

16 15 14 13 12
10 9 8 7 6 5 4 3 2 1

Library of Congress Cataloging-in-Publication Data
Stille, Darlene R.

  The Civil War through photography / Darlene R. Stille.

      p. cm.—(Documenting U.S. history)

  Includes bibliographical references and index.

  ISBN 978-1-4329-6755-0 (hbk.)—ISBN 978-1-4329-6764-2 (pbk.) 1. United States—History—Civil War, 1861-1865—Photography—Juvenile literature. 2. United States—History—Civil War, 1861-1865—Juvenile literature. 3. United States—History—Civil War, 1861-1865—Pictorial works—Juvenile literature. I. Title.

  E468.7.S79 2012

  973.7022'2—dc23   2011038177

Acknowledgments
The author and publishers are grateful to the following for permission to reproduce copyright material:Corbis: p. 15 (© Bettmann); DEFENSEIMAGERY.MIL: pp. 4 (WAR & CONFLICT BOOK), 5 (WAR & CONFLICT BOOK), 18 (WAR & CONFLICT BOOK), 22 (WAR & CONFLICT BOOK), 27 (WAR & CONFLICT BOOK), 31 (WAR & CONFLICT BOOK), 32 (WAR & CONFLICT BOOK), 34 (WAR & CONFLICT BOOK), 35 (WAR & CONFLICT BOOK); Getty Images: pp. 23 (MPI), 37 (Margaret Bourke-White/Time & Life Pictures), 39 (JEFFERSON BERNARDES/AFP), 40 (Tom Williams/Roll Call); Library of Congress Prints and Photographs: pp. 6, 9 bottom, 9 top, 11, 13, 17, 19, 20, 21, 24, 25, 26, 29, 30, 33; Newscom: p. 43 (Kevin Dietsch).

Cover image of the flag of the Pennsylvania Infantry by Mathew Brady reproduced with permission from DEFENSEIMAGERY.MIL (War & Conflict Book). Cover image of Mills House, Charleston, reproduced with permission from DEFENSEIMAGERY.MIL (War& Conflict Book).

Every effort has been made to contact copyright holders of material reproduced in this book. Any omissions will be rectified in subsequent printings if notice is given to the publisher.

Contents

Recording Important Events with Images 4

The Camera Goes to War. 8

A Nation Divided 14

A Picture Record of Battle Sites 18

The Daily Realities of War. 26

The Aftereffects of War 32

Photographing Wars 36

Preserving Photographs 40

Timeline 44

Glossary 46

Find Out More 47

Index 48

Some words are printed in bold, **like this**. You can find out what they mean by looking in the glossary.

Recording Important Events with Images

People create evidence about important events in history. This evidence is often in the form of a document. A document could be a diary, letter, book, or newspaper article. These documents might tell about a conflict, such as the American Civil War (1861–1865). They might tell how people lived during the Civil War or some other time period.

Pictures are also evidence of important events. The pictures could be drawings, paintings, or photographs. Pictures show how people, places, and objects actually looked.

There are two kinds of historical documents and images. They are called **primary sources** and **secondary sources**.

Photographs show how Civil War uniforms looked.

Union soldiers pose with their cannon.

Primary sources

A primary source could be a letter or diary written by an eyewitness. A newspaper article written by a reporter at the scene of a battle or other event is a primary source. A primary source might also be an official report, such as orders from an army general. A constitution of a nation or state is also a primary source.

Pictures as primary sources

A primary source could be a picture. It could be a map drawn by someone to show a path. It could be a drawing or photograph showing how an important person looked. It could be a sketch of a battle being fought. It could be a photograph showing a battlefield before or after the fighting. It could be a photograph of the uniforms that soldiers wore.

Secondary sources

Researchers, writers, and artists study primary sources to create secondary sources. Secondary sources are documents or pictures made by people who did not see a battle or other event happen.

Kinds of secondary sources

History books are secondary sources. A biography of an army general or other leader can be a secondary source. A magazine story or encyclopedia article can be a secondary source.

Paintings or other pictures can be secondary sources. An artist might study Civil War photographs. These primary source photographs can show what leaders looked like. They can show weapons and battlefields. An artist can study these photographs and then paint a picture of the battle, like the one shown here.

This color painting is a secondary source, painted after an event happened. It shows the Battle of Fredericksburg.

Civil War photographs

When historians study the Civil War, they use a variety of primary sources and secondary sources. Some of the most fascinating sources used to study the period are photographs.

Photography was a new kind of technology when the war began. The cameras used at the time of the Civil War could not show action scenes—they would be too blurry. Instead, they show people and places. Photographs at the time of the Civil War were also always in black and white. Color photography had not yet been invented.

But through these photographs, historians can see the faces of the people involved in the war. They can see what the battlefields and destroyed cities truly looked like. By looking back at the photography of the Civil War, we are given an important glimpse of a turning point in U.S. history.

The Camera Goes to War

The first photographs were nothing like the photos of today. They were made by light entering a hole in a wooden box and striking a metal plate. The scene outside the box was reflected by light onto the plate.

The invention of photography

In 1826 a French inventor named Joseph Nicéphore Niépce made the first real photograph. He coated a piece of metal with a chemical that could be changed by light. He had to expose the plate to light for eight hours before an image appeared.

Daguerreotypes and tintypes

In the 1830s, French artist Louis Daguerre made the next improvement in the history of photography. He coated copper plates with silver. His camera exposed the sheets of metal to sunlight coming in through the camera hole.

Know It!

At first, it took up to 40 minutes to make a **daguerreotype**. By the time of the Civil War, it took only about one minute. People being photographed for daguerreotypes or **tintypes** had to remain very still.

1826
French inventor Joseph Nicéphore Niépce makes the first real photograph.

1830s
French artist Louis Daguerre invents the daguerreotype.

Daguerre used a gas called mercury vapor to make an image appear on the plate. He called this type of photo a daguerreotype. Daguerreotypes had sharp, clear images. They were usually portraits, like the one shown on the right.

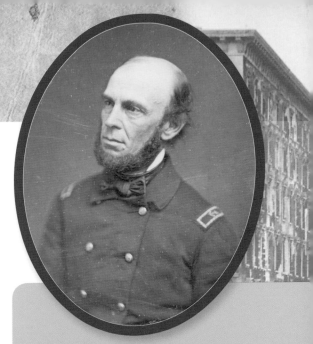

Many Civil War soldiers had their pictures taken in their uniforms. Some had daguerreotypes taken to send to friends and family.

Tintypes were another kind of photograph in the 1800s. People made pictures on thin iron plates. They were sturdier and cheaper than daguerreotypes. These small metal pictures—like this one of a young girl—could easily be carried in a pocket or purse.

By the mid-1800s, daguerreotypes and tintypes were very popular. People used both kinds of photographs for family portraits and portraits of Civil War soldiers.

mid-1850s
The tintype is invented.

A girl in mourning holds a picture of her father, a soldier.

Glass plates and negative prints

Glass plates for taking photographs came into use in the 1850s. The images were very sharp. This was the technology that would be used to photograph the Civil War.

Heavy cameras

Civil War photographers had to carry heavy cameras that looked like wooden boxes. They held the cameras steady by setting them up on wooden legs. The photographers pulled a black cloth over their heads to keep out unwanted light. Then, they opened the camera's **shutter**.

The shutter covered an opening in the camera. The opening usually held a glass lens. The photographer could adjust the lens to get a better picture. Quickly opening and closing the shutter let in just the right amount of light through the lens. A **negative** image was created when light struck the light-sensitive chemicals on the glass. (On a negative, the dark and light areas of an image are reversed.)

Know It!

Civil War cameras could not capture active battle scenes. The pictures of moving horses or soldiers would be very blurry. So, sketch artists went onto battlefields while soldiers were fighting. Their quick sketches captured the action in a way that photography could not at the time.

1850s
Glass plates begin to be used by photographers.

Horse-drawn darkrooms

The photographer could make many **positive** paper prints from a glass plate. But the photographer had to immediately treat the plate with chemicals. The photographer then used light and more chemicals to transfer the image to paper.

These tasks had to be done in complete darkness, in places called **darkrooms**. Civil War photographers had to bring their darkrooms along in wagons drawn by horses, as shown in this image.

Civil War photographers had to bring along their darkrooms on wheels.

Mathew Brady

Mathew Brady was a great U.S. photographer of the mid-1800s. In 1844 he opened his own photography studio in New York City. In 1856 he opened another studio in Washington, D.C.

Brady became best known for his daguerreotype portraits of U.S. leaders, foreign leaders, and other famous people. However, Brady began to have trouble with his eyesight. By 1851 he could not see well enough to use his cameras. He hired other photographers to take the pictures.

Alexander Gardner (1821–1882)

Alexander Gardner was born in Scotland. As an adult, he worked as a photographer for Mathew Brady. As Brady's eyesight grew worse, Gardner helped him. He took over Brady's Washington studio in 1858. After the Civil War broke out, Gardner became one of Brady's Civil War photographers. Gardner took photos of Abraham Lincoln and the people who plotted to kill him. Brady took credit for many photographs taken by Gardner.

1844
Mathew Brady opens his own photography studio in New York City.

1856
Mathew Brady opens a studio in Washington, D.C.

Brady's photos record the war

When the Civil War broke out in 1861, Brady thought it should be recorded with photographs. He thought there should be a complete record of the conflict in pictures. In July 1861, Brady went to the Battle of Bull Run outside Washington, D.C., (see page 18).

Brady then came up with a plan. He hired many photographers. He organized all the photographers to go to different battlefields. He also sent them to camps where soldiers were relaxing. Wherever there were soldiers, there were Brady photographers taking pictures. No matter who took the pictures, they were all labeled "Photography by Brady." Thanks to his efforts, we now have a full photographic record of the war.

General Ambrose Burnside reads a newspaper and photographer Mathew Brady sits near a tree with others at the Army of the Potomac headquarters.

A Nation Divided

Serious differences between the northern and southern parts of the United States led to the Civil War.

North versus South

These differences had a long history. Beginning in the 1600s, **colonists** came to North America from European countries, mainly Great Britain. Some colonists settled in northern parts of the continent. Other colonists settled in southern areas.

The South had a warm climate and a long season for growing crops. Crops such as tobacco and cotton grew well in the South. It took many people to care for these crops. So **slave** traders brought millions of people from Africa against their will and sold them as slaves.

Some enslaved people worked as servants in big Southern mansions. Most performed grueling labor on **plantations** or farm fields (see photograph on page 15).

> ## Know It!
>
> The Republican Party, founded in 1854, grew out of antislavery meetings.

1600s
Colonists from Great Britain and other European countries settle in North America. Over time, differences develop between the North and South.

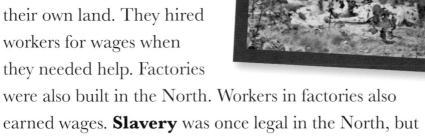

A photo shows an enslaved family in Georgia.

In contrast, in the North the climate was cool. The growing season was short. Most Northerners farmed their own land. They hired workers for wages when they needed help. Factories were also built in the North. Workers in factories also earned wages. **Slavery** was once legal in the North, but it was not a central part of the **economy** there.

A growing problem

The founders of the United States did not solve the slavery problem. Many of them thought of slavery as a "necessary evil."

But over time, many Northerners came to believe that slavery was wrong. Some people wanted slavery outlawed everywhere. People who wanted slavery to be **abolished**, or ended, were called **abolitionists**. There were abolitionists in the South. But most abolitionists were in the North.

1783
The United States becomes an independent country after the colonists win the Revolutionary War, fought against Great Britain. The issue of slavery begins to divide people from the North and South.

The move toward secession

During the 1850s, members of the U.S. Congress argued about slavery. Southern lawmakers believed that slavery should be expanded. Meanwhile, many Northern lawmakers wanted to prevent slavery from spreading to new states or territories. Other lawmakers thought new states or territories should vote on slavery.

States' rights

Southern states feared the **federal** government might outlaw slavery. They thought this move would be against the legal rights of states. They warned that taking away their states' rights would make them **secede**, or leave, the **Union** of states.

Abraham Lincoln (1809–1865)

Abraham Lincoln was president of the United States during the Civil War. Before then, he had been a lawyer, an Illinois state lawmaker, and a U.S. congressman. During the war, Lincoln led Northern forces to victory. He preserved the Union of all the states. He also helped to end slavery. Lincoln became known for great speeches defending democracy. After the Union forces won, an angry Southerner **assassinated** Lincoln in April 1865 (see pages 32–33).

1850s
Members of the U.S. Congress argue about slavery.

1860
Abraham Lincoln is elected president of the United States.

Lincoln is elected

Abraham Lincoln, a Republican, was elected president in 1860. Fearing he would abolish slavery, Southern states withdrew from the Union before his inauguration (official beginning of presidency) in March 1861.

South Carolina was the first state to secede, in December 1860. Mississippi, Florida, Alabama, Georgia, and Louisiana seceded in January 1861. In February 1861, the six states formed what would become known as the **Confederate** States of America. Eventually, 11 states joined this **Confederacy** (see the map).

Eleven Southern slave states made up the Confederate States of America. The Union was made up of 23 Northern states and territories.

Key
- Union free states and territories
- Union slave-holding states
- Confederate states that seceded before the outbreak of war including Indian territory controlled by the Confederates
- Confederate states that seceded after the outbreak of war

0   400   800 kilometers

0   250   500 miles

North / West — East / South

December 1860
South Carolina secedes from the Union.

February 1861
Six seceded states form the Confederate States of America. Eventually there will be 11 total states in the Confederacy.

A Picture Record of Battle Sites

The Civil War began on April 12, 1861. On this day, Southern forces fired on Fort Sumter. This was a fort on an island in the harbor off Charleston, South Carolina, where **federal** troops were stationed.

Fighting at Manassas

The first real battle of the Civil War was at Bull Run (Manassas), a small creek about 30 miles (48 kilometers) from Washington, D.C., in July 1861. People who lived in Washington, D.C., came in horse-drawn buggies to watch. Mathew Brady also arrived to photograph the event. He was almost captured by **Confederate** forces.

Jefferson Davis (1808–1889)

Jefferson Davis was president of the **Confederacy** from 1861 to 1865. He owned a **plantation** in Mississippi and strongly supported **slavery**. Before the war, he had served in Congress and as secretary of war. When the Civil War ended, Davis went to prison for treason (acting against his own country). He was released after two years.

April 12, 1861
Southern forces fire on Fort Sumter, where federal troops are stationed. This is the beginning of the Civil War.

July 1861
Union forces are defeated at the first Battle of Bull Run.

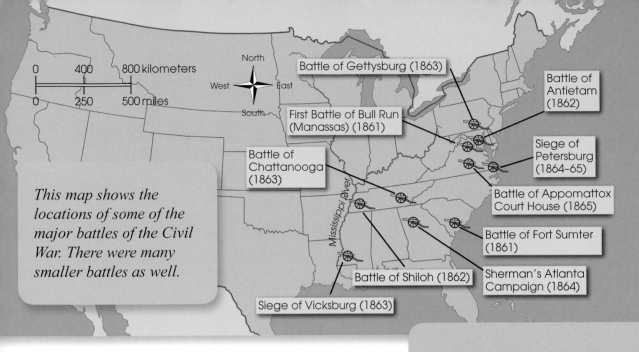

Battle of Gettysburg (1863)

Battle of Antietam (1862)

First Battle of Bull Run (Manassas) (1861)

Siege of Petersburg (1864–65)

Battle of Chattanooga (1863)

Battle of Appomattox Court House (1865)

Mississippi River

Battle of Fort Sumter (1861)

Battle of Shiloh (1862)

Sherman's Atlanta Campaign (1864)

Siege of Vicksburg (1863)

North
West — East
South

| 0 | 400 | 800 kilometers |
| 0 | 250 | 500 miles |

This map shows the locations of some of the major battles of the Civil War. There were many smaller battles as well.

The Confederates, or Southern forces, brought in extra soldiers by train. During the fighting at Manassas, the Union army, as the Northern forces were known, panicked. They fled along with the viewers back to Washington, D.C. Everyone then understood that it would be a bloody war (see the photo on right).

The second Battle of Bull Run was in August 1862. Confederate forces again defeated the Union troops.

This photo shows Bull Run after the first battle.

November 6, 1861
Jefferson Davis becomes president of the Confederate States of America.

August 1862
The second Battle of Bull Run is fought. Confederate forces again defeat the Union troops.

Battles in Northern territory

The Civil War was made up of a long series of bloody battles—many of which were captured by photographers. Most battles in the Civil War were fought in the South (see map on page 19). But two important battles were fought in Northern territory.

The Battle of Antietam (or Sharpsburg)

In September 1862, Confederate General Robert E. Lee (see box) invaded Maryland. The armies fought on September 17, 1862, at Antietam Creek, near Sharpsburg. It was the war's bloodiest day. About 4,700 soldiers were killed. About 19,000 were wounded.

Alexander Gardner captured the aftermath of the Battle of Antietam.

Alexander Gardner became the first photographer to take pictures of dead soldiers. He photographed the battlefield after the Battle of Antietam (see photograph on left).

September 1862
General Lee invades Maryland.

September 17, 1862
The Confederate and Union armies fight at Antietam Creek, near Sharpsburg. It is the war's bloodiest day.

Robert E. Lee (1807–1870)

Historians consider Robert E. Lee one of the greatest generals in U.S. history. Lee graduated from the U.S. Military Academy at West Point, New York. He was an officer in the U.S. Army and later was in charge of West Point. Lee favored slavery but opposed **secession**. He fought for the Confederacy and became commander of the Confederate army.

The Battle of Gettysburg

In June 1863, Lee's army invaded Pennsylvania. Lee wanted to capture Washington, D.C. The armies clashed from July 1 to 3 at a town called Gettysburg. The Confederates began the third day by pounding Union troops with fire.

Meanwhile, Union soldiers rarely fired their cannons. But this was a trick to make Lee think the cannons had been destroyed. When Confederate troops commanded by Confederate general George Pickett charged across a field, Union cannons opened fire. Union forces won. President Lincoln later dedicated part of the battlefield as a cemetery.

June 1863
Lee's army invades Pennsylvania.

July 1–3, 1863
The Battle of Gettysburg is fought. Union forces win.

Battles at sea

Union forces wanted to control the Mississippi River. This would hurt the Southern **economy**, because plantations shipped cotton down the river for trade.

Confederate forces found a way around this. Ships called blockade runners escaped Union gunboats and sailed to Great Britain to trade. After selling cotton, the blockade runners returned with needed supplies.

Ulysses S. Grant (1822–1885)

Ulysses S. Grant became commander of the Union army in 1864. President Lincoln viewed Grant as the fighter he had been looking for. Other Union generals had been cautious and slow to attack. Grant went to Virginia and forced General Lee to surrender. Grant became a national hero. He then served as U.S. president from 1869 to 1877.

1861–1863
Confederate blockade runners bring cotton to Great Britain to trade for needed supplies.

1862–1863
General Grant wins important victories in Kentucky and Tennessee.

22

Siege of Vicksburg

Between 1862 and 1863, the armies also fought fiercely in Kentucky and Tennessee, along rivers leading to the Mississippi. Union general Ulysses S. Grant (see the box) won important victories, including the Battle of Shiloh, in Tennessee. Grant then tried to capture Vicksburg, Mississippi (see map on page 19).

Cannons on the hills of Vicksburg guarded this part of the river, so that Union boats could not pass. But in April 1863, Grant laid **siege** to Vicksburg. He surrounded the city so no one could get in or out. At night, Union gunboats sailed past the cannons and fired on the shore. On July 4, Confederate forces at Vicksburg surrendered (see photograph on right).

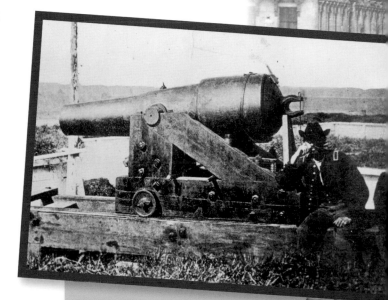

This photo shows a siege cannon from the Battle of Vicksburg on July 4, 1863.

April 1863
General Grant and his forces lay siege to Vicksburg, Mississippi.

July 4, 1863
Confederate forces at Vicksburg surrender.

The South in ruins

After winning the Mississippi River, General Grant invaded Virginia. But Lee's troops fought fierce battles there. Neither side won.

Grant sent other Union generals after Confederate troops in Tennessee and Virginia. One important victory was the Battle of Chattanooga, Tennessee, in November 1863 (see map on page 19). Union general William T. Sherman went after Confederate troops led by General John B. Hood in Georgia. Hood took his troops into Atlanta, Georgia.

Sherman did not want to fight in Atlanta. Instead, he tore up the railroad tracks that allowed trains to bring supplies to Hood's soldiers. Hood and his troops fled. In the summer of 1864, Sherman's troops burned Atlanta (see map on page 19).

Know It!

Many enslaved African Americans fought on the Union side. About 180,000 African Americans (see the photograph) joined the Union army.

May 1864
General Grant invades Virginia. Both sides battle fiercely. Neither side wins. General Sherman invades Georgia.

June 1864
Grant and his troops lay siege to Petersburg, Virginia.

Many buildings in Richmond, Virginia, the Confederate capital, were destroyed by the end of the Civil War.

Sherman's march to the sea

In November and December 1864, Sherman's soldiers marched across Georgia to the Atlantic Ocean. They took food and other supplies they wanted. They burned the rest, along with barns and houses. As the above photograph shows, they left devastation behind them.

Siege of Petersburg

Meanwhile, Grant planned to capture Petersburg, near Richmond, Virginia (see map on page 19). All the railroads that supplied Richmond went through Petersburg. Grant laid siege to the town in June 1864. Fighting there would continue for nine months.

In March 1865, Lee tried to escape, but Union soldiers attacked. Lee surrendered to Grant at a place called Appomattox Court House in April 1865.

September 1, 1864
Sherman captures Atlanta and burns its railroads.

November–December 1864
Sherman burns Atlanta and his troops march to the sea.

April 1865
General Lee surrenders.

The Daily Realities of War

During the four long years the Civil War was fought, the war involved far more than just soldiers in battles. The daily realities of the war ranged from downtime in camps to suffering in hospitals and prisons. Civil War photographs provide insight into this day-to-day side of the war.

Camp life

The armies spent more time in camps than on battlefields. Camp life between battles was boring. Civil War soldiers on both sides played games like checkers and dominos when they were in camp.

Mathew Brady's photographers took pictures of the soldiers in camp. The photos showed the tents the soldiers lived in. They showed how some soldiers cooked their food over campfires. They showed how the soldiers relaxed. The photographs also showed officers at their headquarters. Looking at these photographs serves as a reminder of the real people and life stories behind the soldiers (see photograph).

Troops relaxed when they were not marching or training.

Captured Union soldiers were packed into Andersonville prison.

Prisons and prisoners

Thousands of **Union** and **Confederate** soldiers were taken prisoner during the Civil War. Historians think about 56,000 prisoners died.

One of the worst Confederate camps was Andersonville, in Georgia. The camp was an area inside a stockade, which was a fence made of wooden posts. It was made to hold 10,000 prisoners, but it actually held up to 32,000. About one of every three prisoners there died of disease or starvation (see the above photograph).

Prison camps in the North were also horrible. They were often old barracks (places used to house soldiers) or other buildings. They were not heated in winter. Often the Confederate prisoners had no blankets or warm clothes. Many froze to death.

The sick and wounded

The daily realities for Civil War soldiers often involved sickness and disease. About 500,000 soldiers from both sides were wounded over the course of the war. Many soldiers had to have their arms or legs amputated (cut off) because of bullet and other types of wounds.

Doctors during the Civil War did not yet understand that germs cause **infections**. The doctors did not use clean instruments and bandages. They did not even wash their hands between operations. Medicines like antibiotics, which control the spread of germs, had not been discovered. Many wounds became infected, leading to death.

Know It!

Twice as many soldiers died of disease than of wounds. Dirty food and water in Confederate and Union army camps carried germs. The germs caused diseases like dysentery, measles, pneumonia, tuberculosis, and typhoid. Mosquitoes carried the tiny living things that cause the deadly disease malaria.

Civil War hospitals

Seriously wounded soldiers received emergency treatment at field hospitals. Then, horse-drawn ambulances took them to hospitals away from the fighting in Washington, D.C., Richmond, Virginia, and other places.

But there were not enough hospitals to hold the thousands of sick and wounded soldiers. So the **federal** and Confederate governments set up temporary hospitals in armories (buildings that hold weapons supplies), libraries, schools, houses, and other buildings. This was a time before nurses were trained professionals. Untrained volunteers nursed the sick and wounded.

Photographs like the one shown here reveal the horrors of war. These photographs serve as a reminder of the sacrifice and misery often demanded of soldiers.

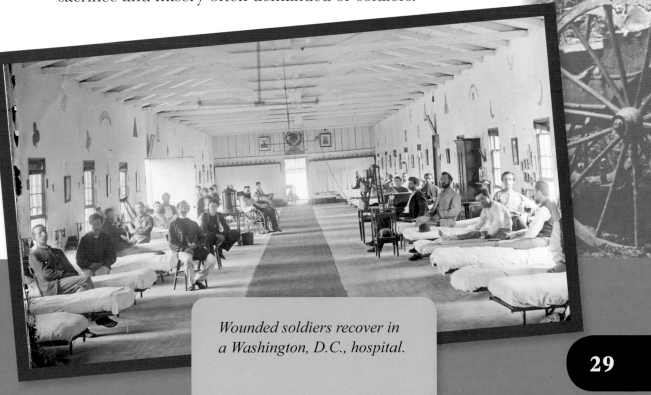

Wounded soldiers recover in a Washington, D.C., hospital.

Women in the Civil War

Women played many key roles in the Civil War, especially in the day-to-day activities. Women served in Union and Confederate camps and on the battlefields.

Washerwomen

Washerwomen, or laundresses, were the only women officially recognized by either army. Washerwomen traveled with the soldiers to do their laundry and other chores. Soldiers who could afford it paid them to keep their underclothes and uniforms clean.

These women were usually poor. Some traveled with their soldier husbands. Some brought their children along. This picture taken by a Civil War photographer provides a record of a washerwoman and her family.

A washerwoman and her family travel with the Union army.

Nurses

Nurses played an especially important role on battlefields and in hospitals. Some, such as Clara Barton (see the box), became heroes for their efforts.

Clara Barton
(1821–1912)

Clara Barton was a volunteer nurse during the Civil War. In 1864 she was appointed superintendent of nurses for one of the Union armies. After the war, on a trip to Switzerland, she learned about the International Committee of the Red Cross. She returned to the United States and founded the American Red Cross.

*Clara Barton used a **tintype** image for her business card. She dropped off a tintype when she visited someone.*

Know It!

Some women disguised themselves as men to fight alongside their brothers or husbands. Others worked as spies. For example, Belle Boyd was a famous Confederate spy. She carried messages through Union lines for Confederate generals. She had many adventures and was arrested several times by Union troops.

The Aftereffects of War

After General Lee surrendered (see page 25), many Americans hoped the country could move toward peace.

Lincoln is assassinated

Tragically, less than a week after the surrender, President Lincoln was **assassinated**. On April 14, 1865, Lincoln and his wife were watching a play at Ford's Theatre in Washington, D.C. An actor named John Wilkes Booth (see the box) went to the president's box seat and shot him in the head. Lincoln was carried to a house across the street. He died early the next morning.

The plotters

Federal troops arrested several people accused of plotting with Booth to murder Lincoln and other officials. A military court sentenced some of the plotters to prison. Four others, including Mary Surratt, were hanged for plotting to kill Lincoln. The plotters had met in Surratt's Washington, D.C., boardinghouse.

John Wilkes Booth (1838–1865)

John Wilkes Booth was a famous actor. He was on the side of the **Confederacy** and supported the right to own **slaves**. After he shot Lincoln, Booth jumped down to the stage. He broke his leg but escaped anyway. Federal soldiers followed Booth. They caught him hiding in a barn in Virginia. He would not surrender. They shot him, and he died.

Crowds in Washington, D.C., watch Lincoln's coffin move down Pennsylvania Avenue toward a railroad station.

Funeral train

Lincoln's coffin traveled 1,700 miles (2,735 kilometers) by train from Washington, D.C., to Lincoln's hometown of Springfield, Illinois. Thousands of saddened people stood along the tracks. The train stopped in 12 cities for memorial services. Photographs of the funeral train capture the solemn mood of the country.

Know It!

Alexander Gardner photographed President Lincoln five days before he was assassinated.

April 14, 1865
Abraham Lincoln is shot while watching a play at Ford's Theatre in Washington, D.C. He dies the next day.

April 21–May 4, 1865
Lincoln's coffin travels to Springfield, Illinois, by train. Mourners line the route.

The costs of war

The Civil War had incredible costs. More than 600,000 soldiers on both sides died during this war. This was more soldiers and sailors than died in all the U.S. wars from the Revolutionary War to the war in Iraq combined. There were also countless injuries. A great leader, Abraham Lincoln, was also lost.

The country itself was also greatly damaged. The states in the former Confederacy suffered the most. Railroads, farms, and cities were in ruins (see photograph below). The whole Southern way of life was destroyed. Bad feelings between North and South lasted into the next century.

Photos such as this one of the Navy Yard in Norfolk, Virginia, show the destruction of the Civil War.

January 1, 1863
Abraham Lincoln issues the Emancipation Proclamation, which leads to the end of slavery.

1865
The 13th Amendment is passed, abolishing slavery.

Positive change

Yet the Civil War led to many positive changes for the country. First, **slavery** was **abolished**. The 13th **Amendment** to the Constitution, passed in 1865, ended this chapter in U.S. history. Millions of former slaves could now live their lives as free Americans (see photograph below).

Second, African American men got the right to vote in 1870, thanks to the 15th Amendment. But this progress would face many challenges in the coming century, as many Southern states found ways to block African Americans at the polls.

Third, the country managed to stay united as a single nation. The Civil War was a tremendous test of strength for the young country. In the next century, the United States would become one of the most powerful countries in the world.

Know It!

On January 1, 1863, Abraham Lincoln issued the Emancipation Proclamation, which was the first step toward the end of slavery.

A photo from the Mathew Brady collection shows African Americans freed after the Civil War.

1870
The 15th Amendment is passed, giving African American men the right to vote.

35

Photographing Wars

Civil War photographers set new standards for capturing images of war and the realities of wartime. Their work still stands as an essential **primary source** record of the time.

New inventions

After the Civil War, in the late 1800s, inventors improved ways to take photographs. Dry plate cameras were smaller than the cameras used during the Civil War. They did not have to be developed in portable **darkrooms**.

When World War I (1914–1918) broke out, there were some early cameras that could take color photographs. Photographers were also able to create some early motion pictures of this war.

Rolls of film

The next great change was the invention of photographic film. Photographers could take pictures on thin rolls of film instead of big, heavy glass plates. Film cameras could be small. Also, film cameras could take pictures faster than older cameras. They could take action shots of people moving.

Margaret Bourke-White, a famous World War II **photojournalist**, took pictures with a camera that used rolls of film.

Photographers during World War II (1939–1945) used film cameras. Color photographs became more common. World War II photographers also made a motion picture record of battle scenes with movie cameras.

Television and video cameras

The invention of television and video cameras was another big step forward. Video photographers filmed action on battlefields. They sent the videotape to television studios. The studios broadcast the pictures.

By the time of the Vietnam War (1955–1975), photographers carried portable video cameras on their shoulders. The photographers went with news reporters into battle areas. The videos of fighting appeared every night on television news programs.

Digital cameras

In the late 1900s, inventors made cameras that did not need any kind of film. **Digital** cameras contain computer chips. They make pictures from computer code. Digital cameras can be plugged into computers. Using photo software, photographers can make their pictures look better. Digital cameras are also smaller and easier to carry around a war zone than earlier cameras had been.

Satellite links to war

While cameras were getting better, **satellites** were being launched. By the 2000s, many communications satellites orbited (circled around) Earth.

News reporters brought satellite dishes to war areas on trucks. Photographers could send their still and moving pictures up to a satellite. The satellite could send the pictures and video to faraway television stations all across Earth. Digital cameras and communications satellites made it possible to send still and moving pictures of war instantly to places on the other side of Earth.

Know It!

A live video picture from a battle area in Afghanistan travels up to an orbiting communications satellite. It then travels down to a television station thousands of miles away at the speed of light.

Today photojournalists capture military action with digital cameras and video cameras.

Photojournalists at work

All the developments in photography since the mid-1800s have given rise to a new profession: photojournalism. A photojournalist helps people understand world events by showing what an event looks like. A photojournalist can use video scenes to show events such as bombs exploding or people running from fighting. Photojournalists can also take still pictures of moments such as leaders in tense talks.

Preserving Photographs

Photographs of the Civil War—and of all events in history—are a precious **primary source**. Experts must take good care of them.

Archivists

Taking good care of historic photographs is the job of a photo **archivist**. An archivist makes a record of each photograph. This record describes the photo, where it came from, and where it is stored. How photographs are stored and cared for depends on the kind of photograph.

A librarian carefully selects a photo of General Lee and his sons, taken after the Civil War, from the archives of the U.S. Library of Congress.

Metal plates

As we have seen, **daguerreotypes** and **tintypes** were popular forms of images during the Civil War period. They are images on metal plates. These plates must be kept away from moisture. Otherwise, they can rust. It is easy to bend the edges of tintypes. And just touching the surface of a daguerreotype can damage it. So tintypes and daguerreotypes must be protected with a piece of glass.

Glass plates and paper prints

The glass plates and paper prints of the Civil War period are also precious. Archivists store glass plate **negatives** so they will not break. They wrap them in paper folders that are free of a kind of chemical called an acid. They use acid-free paper to store both paper photographs and glass plates.

Paul Messier (born 1962)

Paul Messier is an expert on storing photographs printed on paper. Instead of just collecting photos, he collects the kinds of paper used for photo prints. His collection has more than 5,000 different kinds of photo papers. They date from the 1890s up to today. Messier, who works in Boston, Massachusetts, helps date old photographs. He can tell whether a photo is real or fake. He works to conserve important photographs, including many from the Civil War period.

Where are primary source photos stored?

Valuable old photos like those from the Civil War are often stored in libraries and museums. Many Civil War photos are stored in the U.S. National Archives in Washington, D.C. The Library of Congress, in Washington, D.C., also has an impressive collection. Many of these photographs belonged to Mathew Brady.

Brady's collection included his own studio's photographs of the Civil War and photographs that he bought. He had collected about 10,000 photos by the end of the Civil War. He spent his fortune on this project and had hoped to sell the pictures when the war was over. No one, however, wanted to be reminded of that terrible war.

So, Brady lost all his money. In 1875 the U.S. Congress bought all of Brady's Civil War pictures for $25,000. It was not enough to pay Brady's bills, and he died a poor man. Today, however, his collection in the Library of Congress is considered an invaluable part of the library's collection.

Know It!

You do not have to visit Washington, D.C., to see many Civil War photos. Instead, you can also see thousands of Civil War photos on the Library of Congress website (see page 47).

Sources forever

An exhibit shows tintypes and other early images of soldiers from the Civil War collection in the Library of Congress.

Since Brady's time, people have come to value the importance of photographs as primary sources. Photographs have the power to take the viewer back to another time in history. By looking at photographs from the Civil War, we can see the actual faces and places involved in this important moment in history. These primary sources provide a unique link to U.S. history. Thanks to the work of experts and archivists, these photographs will continue to be preserved for future generations.

1875
The U.S. Congress buys Mathew Brady's large collection of Civil War photographs for $25,000.

Timeline

1600s
Colonists from Great Britain and other European countries settle in North America. Over time, differences develop between the North and South.

1783
The United States becomes an independent country after the colonists win the Revolutionary War, fought against Great Britain. The issue of slavery begins to divide people from the North and South.

April 12, 1861
Southern forces fire on Fort Sumter, where federal troops are stationed. This is the beginning of the Civil War.

February 1861
Six seceded states form the Confederate States of America. Eventually there will be 11 total states in the Confederacy.

December 1860
South Carolina secedes from the Union.

July 1861
Union forces are defeated at the first Battle of Bull Run.

November 6, 1861
Jefferson Davis becomes president of the Confederate States of America.

August 1862
The second Battle of Bull Run is fought. Confederate forces again defeat the Union troops.

September 1862
General Lee invades Maryland.

September 1, 1864
Sherman captures Atlanta and burns its railroads.

June 1864
Grant and his troops lay siege to Petersburg, Virginia.

May 1864
General Grant invades Virginia. His forces battle fiercely. Neither side wins. General Sherman invades Georgia.

November 1863
Union forces win the Battle of Chattanooga.

November – December 1864
Sherman burns Atlanta and his troops march to the sea.

April 1865
General Lee surrenders.

April 14, 1865
Abraham Lincoln is shot while watching a play at Ford's Theatre in Washington, D.C. He dies the next day.

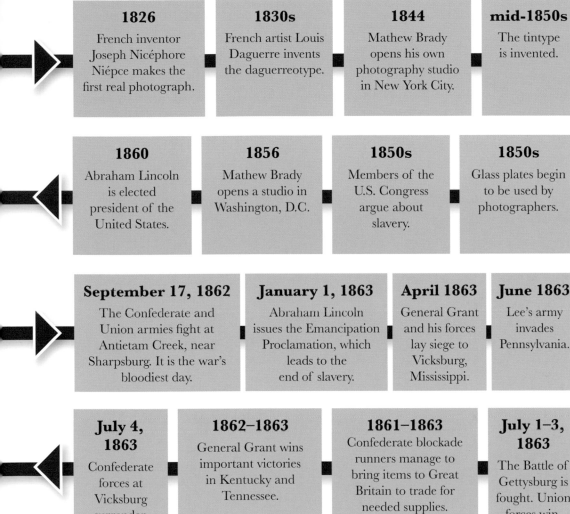

1826
French inventor Joseph Nicéphore Niépce makes the first real photograph.

1830s
French artist Louis Daguerre invents the daguerreotype.

1844
Mathew Brady opens his own photography studio in New York City.

mid-1850s
The tintype is invented.

1860
Abraham Lincoln is elected president of the United States.

1856
Mathew Brady opens a studio in Washington, D.C.

1850s
Members of the U.S. Congress argue about slavery.

1850s
Glass plates begin to be used by photographers.

September 17, 1862
The Confederate and Union armies fight at Antietam Creek, near Sharpsburg. It is the war's bloodiest day.

January 1, 1863
Abraham Lincoln issues the Emancipation Proclamation, which leads to the end of slavery.

April 1863
General Grant and his forces lay siege to Vicksburg, Mississippi.

June 1863
Lee's army invades Pennsylvania.

July 4, 1863
Confederate forces at Vicksburg surrender.

1862–1863
General Grant wins important victories in Kentucky and Tennessee.

1861–1863
Confederate blockade runners manage to bring items to Great Britain to trade for needed supplies.

July 1–3, 1863
The Battle of Gettysburg is fought. Union forces win.

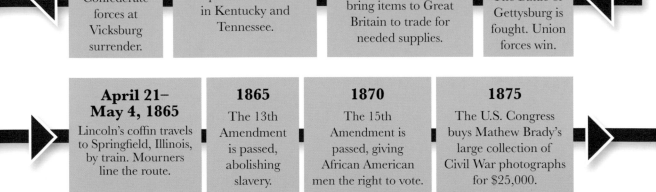

April 21–May 4, 1865
Lincoln's coffin travels to Springfield, Illinois, by train. Mourners line the route.

1865
The 13th Amendment is passed, abolishing slavery.

1870
The 15th Amendment is passed, giving African American men the right to vote.

1875
The U.S. Congress buys Mathew Brady's large collection of Civil War photographs for $25,000.

Glossary

abolish to end something

abolitionist person who wanted to end slavery

amendment change or addition to an official document

archivist person who collects, protects, and preserves records and documents

assassinate murder for political or religious reasons

colonist person who lives in a colony

Confederacy group of 11 states that seceded from the United States during the Civil War

Confederate having to do with the Confederate States of America

daguerreotype silver-coated copper plate treated with mercury vapor

darkroom place that keeps out normal light, to help in developing photographs

digital having to do with computer data

economy system of managing the resources of a country, such as the buying and selling of goods and services

federal having to do with the main government of a country

infection disease caused by germs

negative image showing light and shaded areas in reverse

photojournalist person who records and presents news stories by using pictures

plantation large farm that has crops of coffee, cotton, sugar, or tobacco

positive image showing light and shaded areas as they really appear

primary source document or object made in the past that provides information about a certain time

satellite object that orbits Earth and receives and sends data

secede withdraw from membership in a federation

secession act of seceding, or leaving, a group

secondary source account written by someone who studied primary sources

shutter camera part that opens and closes to let light in

siege to surround a town and cut off supplies, to force surrender

slave person who is forced to work for another person without pay, and who has no rights

slavery practice or system of owning slaves

tintype photographic image on a thin iron sheet

Union name for the Northern states of the United States during the Civil War

Find Out More

Books

Armstrong, Jennifer. *Photo by Brady: A Picture of the Civil War*. New York: Atheneum, 2005.

Fay, Gail. *Battles of the Civil War*. Chicago: Heinemann Library, 2011.

Nemeth, Jason D. *Voices of the Civil War: Stories from the Battlefields*. Mankato, Minn.: Capstone, 2011.

Wisler, G. Clifton. *When Johnny Went Marching: Young Americans Fight the Civil War*. New York: HarperCollins, 2001.

Websites

American Civil War Causes: Kids Zone
www.americancivilwar.com/kids_zone/causes.html
This website about the Civil War includes history, photos, games, and more.

The Civil War for Kids
www.pocanticohills.org/civilwar/cwar.htm
This website is written by and for kids.

Library of Congress: Civil War Photographs
http://memory.loc.gov/ammem/cwphtml/cwphome.html
View the amazing collection of Civil War photographs at the Library of Congress.

Virtual Media Center: The American Civil War
www.sowashco.k12.mn.us/virtualmedia/elementary/civilwar.htm
This website contains primary and secondary sources about the Civil War for students.

Index

abolitionists 15
acids 41
action photographs 7, 10, 36, 37
African Americans 24, 35
amputations 28
archivists 40, 41, 43

Barton, Clara 31
battlefields 4, 6, 7, 10, 13, 21, 29,
  30, 31, 37
Battle of Antietam 20
Battle of Bull Run 13, 18, 19
Battle of Chattanooga 24
Battle of Gettysburg 21
Battle of Shiloh 23
blockade runners 22
Booth, John Wilkes 32
Boyd, Belle 31
Brady, Mathew 12, 13, 18, 26, 42

cameras 7, 8, 10, 36, 37, 38, 39
camps 13, 26, 27, 28, 30
chemicals 8, 10, 11, 41
colonists 14, 15
color photographs 36, 37
computers 38
Confederate States of America 17,
  18, 19, 20, 21, 22, 23, 24,
  27, 28, 29, 30, 31, 32, 34
cotton 14, 22

Daguerre, Louis 8–9
daguerreotypes 8, 9, 12, 41
darkrooms 11, 36
Davis, Jefferson 18, 19
deaths 20, 27, 28, 32, 33, 34
destruction 7, 21, 34
digital cameras 38, 39
diseases 27, 28

Emancipation Proclamation 34, 35

farming 14, 15, 34
field hospitals 29
15th Amendment 35
film 36, 37, 38
Fort Sumter 18

Gardner, Alexander 12, 20, 33
glass plates 10, 11, 36, 41
Grant, Ulysses S. 22, 23, 24, 25
Great Britain 14, 15, 22

historians 7, 21, 27
Hood, John B. 24
hospitals 26, 29, 31

infections 28

Lee, Robert E. 20, 21, 22, 24,
  25, 32
lenses 10
Library of Congress 42
Lincoln, Abraham 12, 16, 17, 21,
  22, 32, 33, 34, 35

maps 5, 17, 19
mercury vapor 9
Messier, Paul 41
museums 42

news reporters 5, 37, 38
Niépce, Joseph Nicéphore 8
nurses 29, 31

paper prints 11, 41
photojournalism 39
Pickett, George 21
plantations 14, 18, 22
plates 8, 9, 10, 11, 36, 41
portraits 9, 12
preservation 40, 41, 43
primary sources 4, 5, 6, 7, 36,
  40, 43
prison camps 26, 27

railroads 24, 25, 33, 34
records 40
Red Cross 31
Revolutionary War 15, 34

satellites 38, 39
secession 16, 17, 21
secondary sources 6, 7
Sherman, William T. 24, 25
shutters 10
Siege of Petersburg 25
Siege of Vicksburg 23
sketches 5, 10
slavery 14, 15, 16, 17, 18, 21, 24,
  32, 34, 35
soldiers 5, 9, 10, 13, 19, 20, 21,
  24, 25, 26, 27, 28, 29,
  30, 34
spies 31
states' rights 16
storage 40, 41, 42
Surratt, Mary 32
surrender 22, 23, 25, 32

television 37, 38
13th Amendment 34, 35
tintypes 8, 9, 41

U.S. Congress 16, 18, 42
U.S. National Archives 42

video 37, 38, 39
Vietnam War 37

women 30, 31
World War I 36
World War II 37